Little Angels

Gervase Phinn

Dalesman

First published in Great Britain 2006
by Dalesman Publishing
an imprint of
Country Publications Limited
The Water Mill, Broughton Hall,
Skipton North Yorkshire BD 2 3 3 AG
www.dalesman.co.uk

Reprinted 2007

ISBN-10: 1-85568-236-2
ISBN-13: 978-1-85568-236-8

Designed by Butler & Tanner Ltd
Colour origination by PPS Grasmere Limited
Printed and bound in China

PUBLISHER'S NOTE
The publisher expresses its gratitude to the children whose
stories and illustrations are reproduced in this book. Copyright is expressly
reserved on their behalf. However, given the nature of the material, it has not
been possible, despite every effort by Gervase Phinn and Country Publications
Ltd, to contact every contributor. In lieu of copyright fees,
Country Publication has made a donation to
the British Dyslexia Association.

CONTENTS

Introduction

For young children, everything around them is new, exciting and colourful, and a source of great wonder. In trying to make sense of the world, they can be charmingly entertaining and sometimes surprisingly profound.

Little Gems, the Dalesman collection of anecdotes, poems and the wise words of children published in 2004, generated a great deal of interest, and I was delighted that so many readers took the time and trouble to send me their own especial favourites. The Dalesman office was inundated with the witty remarks of children, their insightful observations on life, and their amusing and sometimes poignant comments about others – so many, in fact, that I had such a difficult task selecting the ones to publish. So we decided to compile a sequel, *Little Angels*, which I hope you will enjoy dipping into as much as you did with *Little Gems*.

For me, this book has been a labour of love, and I have laughed out loud at the letters, cards, anecdotes and memories you have so kindly sent and allowed me to share with others. I am very grateful to those who offered so much wonderful material but, sadly, space only allows me to publish no more than my own particular favourites. It has not always been possible to credit the author of every piece, for some arrived on the editor's desk without a name, so I extend my thanks to all those who contributed anonymously.

Finally, a word of thanks: to Robert Flanagan, managing director of Dalesman Publishing, for suggesting the original idea and giving me the opportunity to put together this collection; to Mark Whitley, my ever-patient editor who throughout has been good-humoured and supportive; and to my wife Christine who has helped me make the final selection – and done all the typing.

Acknowledgements

The author and publishers would like to thank the pupils and staff of the following schools for their help in providing illustrations: All Saints C of E Primary School, Aston, Sheffield; Beach Grove Elementary School, Delta, British Columbia, Canada; Cayton School, Scarborough; Christ the King RC Primary School, Thornaby, Stockton-on-Tees; Grassington CE (VC) Primary School; Leamington Primary & Nursery School, Sutton in Ashfield; Lydiate Primary School, Liverpool; St Andrew's School, Meads, Eastbourne; Town Field Primary School, Doncaster; Woodthorpe Community Primary School, Sheffield.

The following *Dalesman* readers have kindly contributed to the text: Judith Allott; Jean Bagshaw; Muriel Barber; D Beckett; F Beecroft; Sandra Birch; Sue Black; M C Bonser; Lilian Brooks; Barbara Buckley; Patricia Butcher; D Carter; Jean Chalk; P E Clough; Sam Cottingham; Patricia Devlin; George Evans; Janet Fairs; C Foote; Mrs B E Ford; Eileen Gibb; Andy Gilgunn; Mollie Gooch; J Gough; Alice Haddington; Letitia Halvorsen; Jeanne Hand; Yvonne Helps; Bill Horncastle; Caroline Leckenby; Tony Lilley; Mary Long; David Marshall; John Morley; Stella Morris; Peggy Radcliffe; Margaret Robson; Joan Robertshaw; Hugh Rowland; Anita Simcox; Beryl Smith; Don Smith; Norma Stephenson; A E Swindlehurst; Wyn Thompson; F M Watson; Shirley Webb; Mark Whitley; Maureen Whitley.

Mothers and Fathers

My parents were remarkable people. When I was young I thought that all children had fathers and mothers like mine: loving, funny, generous, ever-supportive. I thought all children had mothers who took out their false teeth and pretended to be witches, and fathers who told wild and wonderful stories, recited monologues ('Albert and the Lion', 'Brown Boots', 'The Green Eye of the Little Yellow God'), and pretended to be monsters and chase them round the living room, growling and grunting.

I thought all children were surrounded with books — fairy tales and fables, nursery rhymes and riddles, Peter Rabbit, the Famous Five, Biggles — and had their own little library of favourites — Treasure Island, Moonfleet, White Fang, Kidnapped, The Thirty-Nine Steps, King Solomon's Mines — and, through reading, inhabited a far-off world of excitement and adventure.

I imagined that all homes had books and stories, music and laughter, courtesy and good manners, honesty and love. It is only now I am older, and have met countless numbers of children in the schools I have visited, that I appreciate just how special my parents were and how hard they tried to bring the four of us up to be honest and decent young people. Now, in later life, I know for sure that the relationship between a child and his or her parents is the most critical influence on that child's life.

When I was a Boy

When I was a boy:
My bunk bed was a pirate ship
That sailed the seven seas,
My sheets they were the silvery sails
That fluttered in the breeze.

I'd dream of clashing cutlasses
And the crack, crack, crack of the gun
And the boom, boom, boom of the cannons
And the heat of the tropical sun.

I'd dream of far-off oceans
And treasure by the ton,
And mountainous waves
And watery graves
And islands in the sun.

My young daughter arrived home with two little friends from down the street.

'Have you come to see the new baby?' I asked.

'No,' said my daughter, 'I told Amy and Hannah they could watch you when you breast feed. They wouldn't believe me when I told them about it.' ―

My little six-year-old son placed his tooth under the pillow for the Tooth Fairy. Since my eyesight is not what it was and his bedroom was dark, I exchanged the tooth for what I thought was a £1 coin. Next morning he came down to breakfast very peeved, holding a one-euro piece, and commented, 'French tooth fairies don't give you as much as the English ones.'

—

Eight-year-old daughter, pointing a little finger at her father before he took her with two friends to Brownies: 'Daddy, before we set off, can we get something straight – no singing in front of my friends.'

—

My young daughter, aged seven, told her younger sister that it was good in the juniors because all the children had 'chicken coops'. Intrigued, I asked her to describe this 'chicken coop'.

'It's where you put your books and things,' she explained. 'It's called a chicken coop.'

She meant 'pigeon hole'.

—

My son, a little Yorkshire tyke, aged ten, lost a tooth and that night placed it under his pillow.

'I can't believe that you still believe in the Tooth Fairy,' I told him.

'I'd believe owt,' he replied, 'if there's money in it.'

—

We were taking our nine-year-old son to the cinema one Saturday evening and caught the bus into town. On the seat opposite us was a youth obviously out clubbing and wearing a garish T-shirt emblazoned with the words 'Oh God, please let me score tonight!'

'What team do you play for?' asked my son innocently.

—

On a flight to Florida my son, aged six, was very excited. He had never been on an aeroplane before and was eager for it to take off. The woman in the next seat was clearly not as keen and closed her eyes as the plane taxied down the runway, engines roaring. My son turned to her and said: 'Let's hope it doesn't crash'.

—

After a display by the dolphins at a zoo, the keeper asked if there was anything the children might like to ask. My young son's question fairly stumped him: 'Don't you think that the dolphins would be happier swimming in the sea instead of doing tricks?'

—

At the pantomime the Ugly Sisters, played by two large and very deep-voiced men, invited children, including my son, onto the stage to ask them questions. When Griselda, one of the sisters, asked him if there was anything he wanted to ask, he looked up and enquired: 'Are you two gay then?'

—

Whilst preparing lengths of wood to be used as flooring in the loft and ably assisted by my four-year-old daughter, she noticed a pile of sawdust where the sawing had taken place.

'Look, daddy,' she cried. 'Crumbs.'

—

My daughter used to spend a long time playing in the bath when she was young. One day, when she eventually got out, her toes were red and wrinkled. She looked at them thoughtfully before announcing. 'I'm all shrinkled.'

—

Son Ian, aged eight, was chattering away fifty to the dozen. I told him to slow down as I couldn't understand what he was saying, adding that he was talking far too quickly.

'I am not talking too quickly,' he told me. 'It's you who are listening too slowly.'

—

I was playing tennis with my seven-year-old daughter when she stopped me in my tracks with the following observation: 'You know, mum, if it wasn't for your face, you'd look about nineteen.'

—

'One day, mummy,' said Lauren, 'I want to get married.'

'Well, he'll be a very lucky boy,' I replied.

'I'm not getting married yet,' she said, horrified. 'You have to be really old and if you pick the wrong person you're stuck with him for the rest of your life.'

'You mean like me and daddy?' I asked jokingly.

'Exactly,' she replied, seriously.

—

My daughter, Lizzie, then aged five: 'Quick mummy, come and look out of the window.'

I looked out to see two dogs mating in the middle of the street.

'Aren't they clever,' says Lizzie. 'They've learnt to do circus tricks.'

—

I was in a family hotel on the Fylde coast, when it was bed-time for one little boy. As his dad approached to carry him off to their room, up the child jumped on his chair, pointed at his father and shouted at the top of his voice: 'Knob head! Knob head! Knob head!' As his embarrassed father swept up the child in his arms and walked past me to the lift, he saw my shocked expression and leaned across to explain.

'It's not what you think,' he said. 'What he was saying was "No bed! No bed! No bed!"'

—

One day I told my small son that the next day, Friday, was pay-day, to which he replied, 'Dad, if you only get paid on Friday, why do you work all those other days.'

—

One year I brought my son, Michael, aged ten, over to the UK on holiday. One day we had bought our tickets and were running for a train. A porter said to us, 'Rushing, are you?'

Michael, with an amazed look on his face said, 'No, we're from Canada.'

—

Dad

22

My son, Adam, aged six, gave me a Father's Day card he had done at school. The teacher had asked the children to write an acrostic where the letter at the beginning of each line, when read downwards, spells the father's name. He wrote:

Watches telly,

Is a supporter of Sheffield Wednesday,

Likes a drink,

Likes to stay in bed,

Is quite fat,

Always spends a long time in the bath,

Makes me smile.

—

My son, aged seven, just would not go to sleep and was told that if he got out of bed again he would be in serious trouble.

'Can I have a drink of water?' he shouted from his bedroom.

'Go to sleep!'

'But can I have a drink of water?'

'No!'

'But I'm thirsty.'

'You should have had a drink before you got into bed.'

'But I'm thirsty.'

'Go to sleep!'

'Pleeeeaaaase.'

'If I come up those stairs, young man, it will be to smack your bottom.'

'Well, when you come up to smack my bottom, will you bring me a glass of water?'

—

I was a month from my thirty-ninth birthday when my youngest son was born. He attended the village school until the age of nine, when he transferred to the middle school in the next village. One day after a week or two he came home highly excited: 'Mum, mum, I have found someone whose mum is older than you!'

———

'My daddy has false teeth,' said my little daughter. 'They come out in a group.'

———

We were on our way back after a day out in Whitby one Sunday and pulled into a market garden outside Pickering.

'What does it mean,' asked my six-year-old, 'if you roger somebody?'

I was taken aback. 'Where did you hear that word?' I asked.

He pointed to the sign in the car park: 'Welcome to Roger Market Garden.'

———

My daughter, Rachel, a bridesmaid at her sister's wedding, was all ears when the vicar asked the bride, 'Do you take this man for better or worse, for richer or poorer, in sickness and in health?'

'Say richer,' whispered Rachel.

———

My son, when we were out for a walk on a very bright, sparkly, frosty morning: 'Look Mummy, the grass has got its lights on.'

———

On our way out for a picnic a few years ago we were passing two reservoirs. I pointed these out to our daughter and told her these were where we got our water.

'Which is the hot one, then?' came the quick reply.

———

My daughter tucked up Kara for the night and was leaving the bedroom when Kara said, 'Put the dark on, Mummy.'

—

Many years ago when our children, Steven and Julia, were about seven and five years of age, we used to take them out most Sundays visiting sights and museums. Afterwards we always had a little quiz on what they had seen.

One Sunday we took the Tube into London, visiting various places including the City, Threadneedle Street and the Stock Exchange. Later we were sitting on the Embankment having an ice cream, when we had the quiz.

I asked, 'What do we call the Old Lady of Threadneedle Street?'

'Maggie Thatcher,' replied Steven.

Grannies and Grandpas

Grannies and grandpas have a very special relationship with their grandchildren. It is self-evident that they have more experience with children, greater understanding and infinitely more patience. They love to see their grand-children but are thankful that they can give them back at the end of the day.

Our family was by no means well off, but my Grandma Mullarkey managed the small amount of money meticulously. She would shop judiciously and was always on the look-out for a bargain. Once, my mother told me, she recalled visiting the fish counter at Sheffield Castle Market. Grandma, looking elegant in her Sunday best, asked for any fish heads, which she would use to make the most delicious soup. 'For the cat,' she told the fishmonger.

'We haven't got a cat,' my mother piped up with all the honesty of the young child.

'Yes we have,' said grandma, giving her a knowing look and a wink.

'No we haven't,' persisted my mother, to all in earshot. 'My mum boils up the fish heads in a big pot over the fire for our tea.'

Letter to Grannie and Grampa

Dear Grannie and Grampa,
Mother's come out in a rash,
Father's got the mumps,
Richard's got a tummy ache,
Dominic's got lumps.
Mum's got German measles,
But there's nothing wrong with me,
And I cannot wait for Sunday,
When you're coming round for tea.

Interrogation in the Nursery

Infant: What's that on your face?
Inspector: It's a moustache.
Infant. Can I have one?
Inspector: No, little girls don't have moustaches.
Infant: Can I have one when I grow up?
Inspector: No, ladies don't have moustaches either.
Infant: Well, my grannie's got one.

I was reading a pop-up picture book about animals with my young granddaughter, aged three, which made an animal noise appropriate to the creature on the page. With each sound I asked her to guess what creature she thought it might be. The tiger snarled, the bison grunted and the monkey chattered. I paused to blow my nose. 'Elephant,' she cried.

—

I was looking in the mirror and observed, speaking to my nine-year-old granddaughter, that I had lots of wrinkles and that I perhaps needed a facelift.

'No, granny,' she exclaimed. 'Don't go to one of the drastic surgeons.'

———

When I asked my young grandson what Father Christmas was bringing him for Christmas, he shouted, 'A BIKE! I'M GETTING A BIKE!'

'You have no need to shout,' I told him, 'Father Christmas is not deaf, you know.'

'I know,' he replied, 'but daddy's upstairs and he might not hear me.'

———

While shopping with my granddaughter, aged four, we went into a café for a cup of tea and a sandwich. When the beautifully garnished sandwiches arrived, my granddaughter announced in a very loud voice: 'I am not eating them! They are full of weeds.'

———

Little Robert, my grandson, aged four, was looking curiously at trays of bedding plants waiting to be planted in the garden. The trays, with the exception of one, were clearly labelled.

'Grandma, what are those flowers called?' he asked.

'Oh dear, Robert,' I said as I touched my brow, 'I can't remember. It's at the back of my mind.'

'Well, grandma,' he suggested, 'just tip your head forward and it might come out.'

———

My granddaughters Georgina and Jessica, aged four, asked if they could go outside to play. 'You go out first, granddad,' said Georgina. 'You'll be able to tell if it's raining because you're bald.'

—

In a doctor's surgery my grandson approached an elderly man in a wheelchair and asked him, 'Can you do wheelies in that?'

—

Recently my grandson's teacher was complimenting him on his work and asked, 'Who do you take after?'

My grandson replied, 'That's easy. I take after my grandfather – he used to be intelligent.'

—

The time had arrived when I had to say goodbye to my son and his family, and return to my home in Australia, after spending a wonderful holiday with them. It was a very emotional time so I decided to make my departures when they were busily eating lunch. I was determined to leave without them knowing that my heart was near to breaking.

'Well,' I said, in a trembling voice, 'I've sewn all the name tags on your school clothes, I've tidied your rooms, I've made lunch and now it's time for me to say goodbye. Is there anything you want to say before I go?'

'Could you pass the tomato sauce please?' asked Edward, aged six.

—

On grandma's seventieth birthday, all the family gathered around the table for a celebration meal. The highlight was when William, aged ten, brought in the beautifully iced and

33

grandma

grandad

decorated birthday cake. Grandma, duly touched, asked, looking towards her daughter with love and gratitude, 'And who did all the hard work with the cake?'

'Marks and Spencer,' replied William.

—

Jamie's great-grandfather was in the Second World War and distinguished himself fighting in the Western Desert. When he came out of the army he joined the fire service, and there too took on a dangerous and difficult job of work. On several occasions he risked his own life. When he retired he had a triple heart bypass and survived prostate cancer.

At a children's playground, Jamie asked his great-grandfather if he would like to go down the slide and, when he received the reply that it was not for him, Jamie shook his head, looked at his great-grandfather pityingly, and said, 'Come on great-gramps, don't be such a wimp.'

—

A few years ago the family were at my mother's for her birthday, when out of the blue my young nephew, who had been learning about evolution at school, asked: 'Nanna, did you use to be a monkey?'

—

I have fine surface veins on the back of my legs and when I took my three-year-old grandson swimming his comments were, 'Who has been drawing maps on the back of your legs, grandma?'

—

Joshua, aged seven: 'Grandma, your hands feel like pizza dough.'

—

Jake was around two years old and loved to play hide-and-seek, his favourite hiding place being behind the long curtains. It was just before Christmas and he had been taken by his grandmother to the children's Christingle service at her local church. The service was about to start and the vicar hurried down the aisle and disappeared into the vestry, behind a curtain. This did not go unnoticed by Jake, and he was out of his seat in a flash and racing down the aisle.

'Come on, nanna,' he shouted. 'Hiding.'

———

As I was reading the story of *Peter Pan* to my granddaughter Emma, aged four, she asked: 'Granddad, what did they call Captain Hook before he lost his arm?'

———

My grandson and I were playing with his Lego on the carpet, and I had my head down over the piece I was building. 'Granddad,' my grandson said, 'do you know that the top of your head is growing through your hair?'

———

Foolishly I was persuaded by my grandson to go down the water chute at a leisure centre. Being 'amply proportioned', I got stuck halfway down. It was only with the help of the teenager sliding down behind me, who crashed into me and dislodged me, that I managed to make it to the bottom. I was catapulted into the water with the very embarrassed young man on top of me. Surfacing, I found the attendant blowing his whistle shrilly and ordering me out. My grandson, who had been watching proceedings, said as I staggered towards him, wet, bedraggled and shame-faced, 'Can you do that again, grannie?'

———

My grandsons Alister and Fraser, aged six and seven, were playing soldiers at war. I told them I had lived through World War Two when a little girl, explaining why I had to wear gas masks and ear plugs, and also having to go into air-raid shelters when German planes came over to drop bombs. They both stood looking at me in awe, then Fraser asked, 'But grandma, why aren't you dead?'

———

I was singing in the bathroom when my grandson's head appeared about the door. He is seven and has just started at a rather posh preparatory school.

'Grandpa,' he said, 'cut out the singin', you're doin' mi 'ead in.'

———

My young grandson was suffering from a bout of low self-esteem. His dad was doing his best to convince him that he was indeed a bright, clever and popular young man, but wasn't getting through. Eventually his dad asked: 'Have I ever lied to you?'

'Well,' Jonathan replied, 'you did about Father Christmas.'

———

My great-niece wanted to know how old I was.

'I don't know,' I said mischievously.

'You ought to know how old you are,' she said. ' I know how old I am.'

'Well,' I said, 'I must have forgotten.'

'Well, look in your knickers, granny,' she said.

'Look in my knickers,' I repeated intrigued, 'and how will that help?'

'It tells you how old you are on the label. Mine says for a 5–7 year old.'

———

I was dancing to 'Chirpy, Chirpy, Cheep, Cheep' at the reception after my grandson's wedding and as I left the floor, I was taken aside by my very serious great-grandson. 'Granny,' he said, 'a bit of advice. You're too old for that sort of thing.'

—

My son had been looking at some old black-and-white family photographs. When he next saw his granddad he asked, 'Were you alive, granddad, when the world was black and white?'

—

This exchange took place recently between my three-year-old grandson Adam and me when looking in a drawer in our house for a favourite toy:

'Oh dear, Adam, this drawer is in an awful muddle – I expect the toys in your room are all nice and tidy.'

Adam, in all seriousness, 'Oh no, granny, our house is a mess – just like yours.'

—

My young granddaughter, Amy, was in the back of my car one day when I, forgetting for a moment that she was with me, referred to the driver in front of me as 'a prat'.

Amy then asked, 'And is the lady with him Mrs Prat?'

—

A few gems from the grandchildren:

'Mummy puts rhododendron under her arms.'

'Oh dear, every time granddad gets a good idea it makes life difficult.'

'We've been to the theatre to see the Sugar Lump Fairy.'

'Aunty Di hasn't any children of her own so she has to use me.'

'Aren't I lucky to have a nan and granddad who aren't dead.'

—

My friend's granddaughter was looking at her intently, then said, 'You should use some of that wrinkle cream advertised on the telly. I'll bring you some,' which she did the next time she called. A few days later her grandma came under close scrutiny again.

'Are you still using that cream, grandma?'

'Yes,' she answered.

'Doesn't work very well, does it?' came the honest reply.

—

On the telephone with my granddaughter, aged four and a half.

Lauren: Happy birthday, Pappa.

Pappa: Thank you, Lauren.

Lauren: How old are you today?

Pappa: I'm sixty-nine. I expect that seems very old to you.

Lauren (without hesitation): That's not very old, Pappa – it's just really grown-up.

—

My granddaughter Jenny, aged six, painted a colourful picture and brought it to show me.

'Why, that's lovely, Jenny. What is it?' I said.

She gave me a scathing and rather pitying look, and replied 'A *real* artist doesn't have to say what it is, Grandma.'

—

My grandson had just started school and was very fond of his diary. One entry was: 'My grandma has cat biscuits and shoe polish for breakfast.' He was referring to the latest breakfast cereals and my Marmite on toast.

—

A few years ago my wife and I, accompanied by our four-year-old grandson, were walking into the town centre by way of the parish church. The path through the churchyard is somewhat restricted and, to maximise the available space, old gravestones have been laid flat alongside the single-slab paving stones.

Understandably our grandson was about to walk on the gravestones when we stopped him, saying they belonged to people who had died and were buried in the churchyard.

'What are gravestones?' he asked. We replied they were in remembrance of those people, and written on the stones were their names, ages and often kind messages and verses were included in honour of the deceased.

'Oh, like get-well-soon cards?' our grandson rejoined.

–

Giving my granddaughter, aged three, a piggyback home, she said: 'Granddad, when are you going to get a proper job – not this teaching thing?' I was headteacher of a comprehensive school at the time.

Uncles and Aunts

My Auntie Nora and my mother trained as nurses. Nora was quite a beauty and had a succession of eligible beaus. At the time when she was sister-in-charge of the casualty department at Doncaster Royal Infirmary she was 'walking out' with a doctor, much to the delight of my grand-mother, who had very high hopes for her children.

Auntie Nora was a great storyteller. She would tell tales about when she was training to be a nurse. Mischievous doctors would send her up to ward nine for a couple of Fallopian tubes. Once, the surgeon in the operating theatre asked her to fetch sister's coat. Thinking it was another ruse, my aunt refused. The surgeon exploded and demanded that she fetch sister's coat as instructed. 'Do as you are told, nurse!' ordered the theatre sister, as red-faced and furious as the surgeon. My aunt scurried off and returned with sister's coat. The surgeon bit his lip, looked heavenwards and, controlling his temper, informed my aunt it was the cystoscope which he required.

Uncle Alex was dad's elder brother. He was a highly decorated officer in the Royal Air Force and flew as a navigator during the War. I have his eight medals, which include the MBE, on my wall. Uncle Alex looked and spoke like a character out of my *Biggles* books. He was tall and lithe, with a great ginger handlebar moustache and hands like spades. He would appear at the door, with his brown canvas bag, stay for a few days and then depart. Once he arrived in the early morning and climbed though a window to gain entry. He then settled down on the settee in the front room only to be confronted later by my father brandishing a poker and assuming he had burglars.

It was Uncle Alec who attempted to show me how to play cricket.

Unlucky Uncle Alec

Unlucky Uncle Alec
While one day playing cricket,
Saw a four-leaf clover
And thought that he would pick it.
As he bent down towards the ground,
To pluck the lucky leaf,
The cricket ball flew through the air
And knocked out all his teeth.
He shouted 'Drat!' and dropped the bat,
Which landed on his toes,
It bounced back up and cracked his chin,
Then smacked him on the nose.
Smeared in blood and caked in mud,
He said, 'I'm glad that's over,'
Then with a sigh, he held up high,
His lucky four-leaf clover.

When my young niece, Jade, aged six, was visiting, she was very taken with my new outfit.

'You look really nice, Auntie Christine,' she said sweetly.

'Thank you, Jade,' I said, 'that's very nice of you to say.'

'And I really really like your dress.'

'Do you?'

'Mummy's got some curtains like it.'

—

49

Having spent yet another weekend with his two old aunties in the country while his parents were away, Little Sam was asked to say thank you.

'Go on, Sam, say "thank you for having me"', urged his mother.

Sam reluctantly obliged. Aunty Dora patted his little head and said, 'You'll come and see us again, won't you?', to which Sam replied, 'Only if I'm forced!'

———

'You might not be as tall as daddy,' said my young son to his Uncle Michael, 'but you're a lot, lot wider.'

———

Aunty was watching the funeral service of Sir Winston Churchill on the television with her little nephew. As the coffin was carried into the church he suddenly said: 'I know what they are going to do now. They're going to open the box.'

———

My young nephew, all of eight, came to visit. His father is a barrister, his mother a solicitor. I had lost my glasses, and searched high and low without success.

'Now, let's think about this logically,' he said seriously. 'Can you recall where you last had them?'

He clearly was to follow in his parents' footsteps.

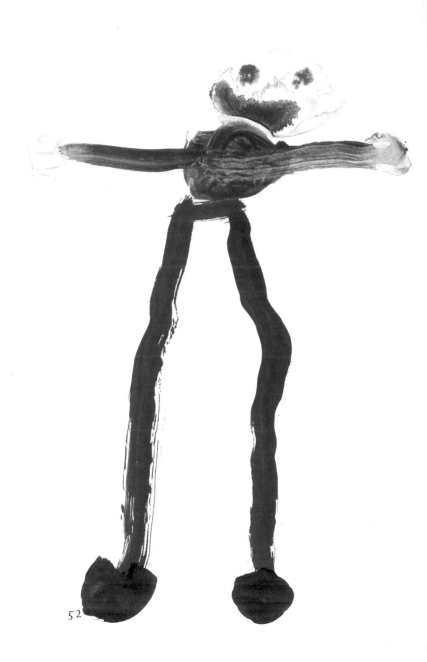

52

Friends and Neighbours

When I was growing up in Rotherham, Mr Evans, our next-door neighbour, was incredibly bow legged and waddled down his garden path, much to our amusement. Dad told me the reason for Mr Evans' unusual gait. Before I was born, Mrs Evans had been painting the bathroom windowsills. She cleaned her brush in turpentine substitute and then poured the remains of the very inflammable liquid down the toilet. Mr Evans, so dad related, was wont to sit on the toilet reading his paper and enjoying his pipe. You might predict the outcome that particular morning. Mrs Evans had not flushed the toilet so, when her poor unsuspecting husband tapped the smouldering remains of his pipe down between his legs and into the toilet bowl, there was a great flash followed by terrible screams. The ambulance duly arrived but, when a distraught Mrs Evans explained how the unfortunate casualty had suffered such severe burns to his nether regions, the ambulance men, halfway down the stairs, became convulsed with laughter and dropped the stretcher, causing Mr Evans to tumble out and break both legs. Hence, dad explained, the poor man's unusual way of walking.

Our other neighbour Mrs Rogers frequently popped in for a cup of tea and a chat with mum, and I – a little boy of six or seven – would sit playing with my Lego or train set, listening. Sometimes the conversation would be *sotto voce* when the topic was not for 'little ears' and I had to strain to listen. 'He's a wolf in sheep's clothing, that one,' Mrs Rogers would say or 'She's no better than she should be – all fur coat and no knickers'. I've always had a great deal to say, but I have also been a keen listener and a sharp observer of people. I suppose writers have to be magpies, collecting gobbets of conversation, little gems of language, quirks of character, accents and mannerisms, because that is from where they get the material for their stories and poems.

When my neighbour's garden fence blew down in the wind, crushing my flowers and smashing all the glass in my cold frame, I was angry and upset. Our grandson Tom, all of six years old, put his hands on his hips and shook his little head before saying, 'You know what I always say, granddad, it's not the end of the world.'

—

When a friend of mine died, I told my small grandson how much I would miss her and how I wished she were still alive. He watched me as I wrote a black-edged 'In Memoriam' card, adding 'RIP' after her name.

'What does 'RIP' mean, grannie?' he asked.

'Each letter stands for a word,' I told him.

'Return if possible?' he asked.

—

'What's a coot?' my little boy asked our neighbour, who was mowing the lawn at the front of his house.

'It's a bird, I think,' said Mr Martin. 'Why do you want to know?'

'My dad says you're like a coot.'

'Are you sure he said coot?' asked our neighbour, intrigued.

'Well, he said you were as bald as one.'

—

Mr Evans, our next-door neighbour, was feeling rather down when his dog, Jessie, died. My son, aged six, trying to cheer him up, used a favourite expression of his grandpa's ('Keep your pecker up') but didn't quite get it right. He told a rather surprised Mr Evans to 'Keep your plonker up'.

—

A friend of mine works in the local library in the children's section. Young people frequently come in asking for a book but they are not certain of the title. She's been asked for Harry Potter's 'Gobbit of Fire' and a version of 'Willy Wonker and the Chocolate Factory' (I will leave it to your imagination as to what the child asked for).

A very popular series used to be 'Nancy Drew and the Hardy Boys'. One child asked her, 'Have you any books about "Hardy Drew and the Nancy Boys"?'

Another popular series with young girls was the 'Sweet Dreams Series'. One innocent asked my friend if there were any books in the 'Wet Dreams Series'.

—

Little Kevin kept asking his mum to take him to the toilet. Mum was talking to her friends so didn't hear him. I said I would take him and Kevin asked, 'OK, but can *you* wipe bums?'

—

My next door neighbour's little girl, Juliet, aged eight, came home after visiting her new baby brother in hospital. She told me: 'He won't be home yet because he's very small and has to be kept in an incinerator.'

—

I am seventy-seven, and was mowing my lawn at the front of the house when the little boy whose parents had just moved in next door asked me, 'Have you a bike?'

'I have,' I replied.

'So do you want to come out to play then?'

I felt seventy years younger.

—

I once had a spell as a door-to-door salesman. In my first inexperienced days I called at one house where a small boy opened the door to my knock.

'Is there no one else in?' I asked.

'Yes, my sister,' said the boy brightly.

'Perhaps I could see her,' I said.

He disappeared and did not return for several minutes. Then I heard a voice calling,

'You'd better come in, mister, I can't lift her out of the playpen myself.'

Teachers and Preachers

I am five. The photograph shows a chubby little boy with a round, pale face, a mop of black hair and large eyes, sitting on the back step of the house in Richard Road, taken just before he sets off for his first day at school. I am wearing a crisp white shirt and little tartan clip-on tie, short trousers which I eventually grow into, socks pulled up to the dimpled knees and large polished black shoes. I do not look at all happy. In fact, I seem on the verge of tears.

Broom Valley Infant School appeared to a small boy of five as a vast, cold and frightening castle of a building with its huge square metal-framed windows and endless echoey corridors, shiny green tiles, hard wooden floors, and the oppressive smell of stale cabbage and floor polish. It was a daunting place and on my first day, so my mother told me years later when my own children started school, I screamed and shouted, tugged and writhed as she held my small hand firmly in hers on our way to the entrance. I hated it, and wanted to go home and sit at the table in the kitchen, and help my mother make gingerbread men and listen to her stories. When I saw her head for the door I thought I would be abandoned forever and couldn't be consoled. 'I want to go home!' I cried. 'I want to go home!' But I was made to stay and I spent the whole morning whimpering in a corner, resisting the kind attentions of Miss Greenhalgh, the infant teacher. At morning playtime I couldn't be coaxed to eat the biscuit or drink the milk on offer and continued to sniffle and whimper.

But by lunchtime I had become intrigued and soon dried my tears. Just before lunch, Miss Greenhalgh opened a large coloured picture book and began to read. I loved books, and the bedtime routine was my mother or father or sister snuggling up with me to read. I knew all the nursery rhymes and the fairy stories and, although I couldn't read, I knew if a word was changed or a bit missed out and would tell the reader so. When Miss Greenhalgh opened the book on that first morning, I stopped the sniffling and listened. She looked to me like someone out of the pages of a fairy tale: long golden hair like Rapunzel's, large blue eyes like Snow White's, and such a gentle voice and lovely smile like Sleeping Beauty's. When she started reading the story, I was completely captivated. The following morning I wolfed down my breakfast, keen to get back to school and Miss Greenhalgh.

Tantrum!

'I'll stamp my feet!
I'll make a fuss!
I'll squeal and screech and shout!
I'll kick my legs!
I'll bang my head!
I'll wave my hands about!
I'll bring the roof down with the noise!
I'll shriek and scream and howl!
I'll cry and yell and bellow and bawl!
I'll wail and whoop and yowl!
I just won't go to school today,
With all the girls and boys,
I want to stay at home instead,
And play with all my toys.'

'Now come along,' his mother said,
'And do not act the fool.
Get out of bed, you sleepy head
You're headteacher of the school!'

The vicar caught a boy smoking.
    'Do you know where little boys who smoke go to?' he asked .
    'Aye,' replied the boy, 'up top o' t' ginnel.'

—

Our lady curate, who usually goes into the local primary school in her normal clothes except for her collar, had brought the class of eight-year-olds into church to demonstrate a baptism complete with mum and baby. For this occasion she had put on her cassock and she asked the children if they could see anything different about her. The first little boy put up his hand and said, 'Yes, you are wearing your God suit.'

—

A vicar, with the word 'grace' in mind, asked the children, 'Does anyone know what is said before you eat?'

'I know what my dad says,' said a child. '"Go easy on the butter".'

—

The parish priest was visiting and, before leaving, asked in a rather hushed voice if he could use the toilet. As he headed for the door my little daughter, Anna, aged six, shouted after him: 'And don't forget to put the seat down and flush the toilet when you've finished.'

—

When my sister was about four we had a surprise visit from our new priest. My mum went to make a cup of tea for him and made sure that the bathroom was tidy with a clean towel. My sister used the loo later and, running into the lounge, she said in a big voice, 'Mum, who owns the new towel in the bathroom?'

—

All the same all the same in sunshine and the rain. No matter who you are you now god loves us all the same

Dominic was all ready to go to church for his first Holy Communion, dressed in pristine white shirt, black bow tie, carefully pressed shorts, grey socks and polished black shoes.

'You look lovely, darling,' cooed granny, 'quite the little angel in your smart new outfit.'

'Yes,' he replied scowling, 'and my dad says it was a real bugger to iron.'

—

I took my class of seven-year-olds to the local Roman Catholic church in preparation for their first Holy Communion. The priest explained about the responses to his prayers during mass and hoped that the children would speak them loudly and clearly – particularly the final response, 'Thanks be to God'. At the mass one small boy, with a particularly loud and resonant voice, heard the priest tell the congregation to 'Go in peace, to love and serve the Lord', and he sat up smartly and responded with 'Thank Christ for that!'

—

'In the Bible,' said the Methodist minister, talking to a group of children in assembly, 'there is a very famous sentence, "He who lives by the sword will …" Can anyone complete it for me?'

One bright spark piped up, 'Will get shot by him who has a gun.'

—

The rural dean visited our school and told them he was really a sort of vicar.

'Can anyone tell me anything about vicars?' he asked.

'It rhymes with knickers,' said a child.

—

The priest processed down the aisle at mass in his embroidered cope.

'I like the dress,' said my young granddaughter.

—

A little boy arrived at our playgroup in Snaith, having recently moved with his family. His father had started work at the large Drax power station and he decided to take his young son to show him how it worked, As they approached the great cooling towers the child said: 'Ooooh, look daddy, a cloud factory.'

—

'Mummy,' said Bethany as she observed me just before I was to give birth to her brother. 'You're getting really fat.'

'I know, darling,' I replied, patting my stomach. 'That's because I have a baby in my tummy.'

She had a good look at my behind. 'Well, what have you got in your bottom?'

—

The teacher read the story of 'Little Red Riding Hood' and then asked the children to write the story in their own words. My six-year-old wrote that, 'Little Red Riding Hood had bright red tits.' She explained to the surprised teacher that she meant 'tights'.

—

Two infants talking in the school canteen over lunch.

'What have you got in your lunch box?'

'Crisps and egg sandwiches. What have you got?'

'Meat sandwiches and a yoghurt.'

'What's yoghurt?'

'It's like strawberry-flavoured snot.'

—

74

The headteacher was telling the children in assembly that Jesus said 'Love thy neighbour' and that violence was wrong. He spoke at length about the importance of being kind and considerate to each other. When the children arrived back at my classroom two little boys got in a fight.

'What did the headteacher just say about being kind and considerate to each other and violence being wrong?' I demanded as I pulled them apart.

Before they could respond, Britney, an angelic-looking girl, came forward and said, 'Give them a really good smack, miss! That'll stop them.'

—

The English language is a tricky business. The teacher explained to the infants that the two letters 'c' and 'h' when put together make the sound 'ch' as in 'chain', 'chair', 'chop' and 'champion'. She asked the children to suggest words with the initial sound 'ch'.

'Choolip,' announced a child.

—

The teacher asked the children to tell her something that had happened during their summer holidays which was interesting.

'When we were on the ferry to France,' volunteered one small girl sweetly, 'my granddad threw up into the wind.'

—

A six-year-old pupil in our school is well known for not being quite together when it comes to pens and ink. He is possibly a little on the clumsy side but seems to have learnt to live with it. One day his teacher, Mr Hook, was trying to fit a new cartridge into an ink pen belonging to another pupil who had been having difficulty. The teacher pushed the cartridge into the pen, and ink squirted out all over his desk and hands. Our six-year-old friend had been watching and smiled at the teacher, saying, 'Welcome to my world, Mr Hook.'

—

A teacher was giving the children a talk on hygiene and asked what the children did before they went to bed at night. She was expecting the predictable answers: 'wash', 'bath', 'clean your teeth', etc. One little boy raised his hand.

'Please, miss,' he announced. 'My dad pees in the sink.'

—

When I went to school I had never heard of PE – it was always gym. My son, Andrew, started school in 1964 and one day I asked him what he had been doing. Imagine my shock when he said, 'Peeing in the playground.' I was greatly relieved when I found out they had been doing their exercises outside.

—

Returning home from school, my daughter, Heather, aged seven, asked me if Jesus really was a Jew. When I told her he was, she looked puzzled.

'I always thought he was a Methodist, like us,' she said.

—

After singing 'Daisy, Daisy,' I asked my class, 'Does anyone know what they call a bicycle made for two?' I was expecting the answer 'tandem', but one boy, aged seven, answered, 'Is it a condom, miss?'

—

During the visit of the school inspector, who sat at the back of the infant classroom watching proceedings, the child sitting next to him continued to make rather loud and flatulent noises, with the accompanying smells. Finally the school inspector had had enough and asked the child to desist.

'For your information,' said the child boldly, 'I've got irritable bowel syndrome.'

—

'And what do you think a homeopath does?' the teacher asked my eleven-year-old son. 'Does he kill gay people?' came the reply.

—

A teacher was explaining about figurative language to the children, that winter is sometimes referred to as a person – 'Winter with his cold white hands and icy breath'. Thinking of spring, she asked, 'And what comes in like a lion and goes out like a lamb?'

'My dad,' replied a small boy.

—

'Can you move me from this table, miss?' asked an infant in my class, 'John's a bad effluence on me.'

—

Two little boys had got into a playground scrap.

'How did it start?' asked the headteacher.

'It started when John kicked me back.'

—

I was interviewing a prospective pupil, whose parents had applied to send their daughter to our preparatory school. In front of my desk sat the nervous mother and her eight-year-old daughter, who didn't look at all worried by the ordeal.

'And what do you like doing?' I asked.

'I like music,' replied the child, 'and I play the piano.'

'She's got grade four piano,' added her mother proudly.

'And I like reading.'

'She reads a book a week,' said the mother.

'And swimming,' said the child.

'She has medals,' added the mother.

'And,' – the girl looked at her mother – 'what sort of pro-grammes do I like to watch on the television?'

—

Infant commenting on Prince Charming touring his realm with the crystal slipper in search of the love of his life: 'Well, I wouldn't try on Cinderella's slipper. I might get a verruca.'

—

'How old are you, Miss?' asked a seven-year-old. I replied that I was twenty-one. 'I bet my grandma would like her birthday to go backwards like yours,' he replied.

—

The children had been across to the parish church for their 'Wednesday in Lent' service. The vicar had been talking about caring for one another, being kind, helpful, considerate and being friendly together – no fighting, no squabbling, all living together as a happy family.

Miss Richardson, the infants' teacher, was bringing up the tail end of the crocodile and on arrival in the classroom was

met with the sight of two seven-year-old boys rolling about the floor and knocking the daylights out of each other. She hauled them up by their coat collars and demanded, 'What do you mean by behaviour like this? You've just been to church and the vicar has been talking about being kind and helpful and friendly, and I come into the room and find you carrying on in this dreadful manner. What have you got to say for yourselves?'

She was reading the riot act in no uncertain manner when another seven-year-old, not a particular angel himself, sidled up to her and said in awed tones, 'Eeeh, Mrs Richardson, won't God be mad!'

—

Lucy, aged six, had drawn a picture of Mary, Joseph, baby Jesus and the donkey on their way from Bethlehem. On the back of the donkey was a huge hairy creature with a grinning face.

'What's that?' asked the teacher.

'The flea,' replied Lucy.

The child had added a completely new meaning to the phrase, 'Take your wife and flee to Egypt.'

—

I was showing the children some pictures of the Nativity scene painted by famous artists.

'It must have been a bit crowded in the stable, miss, what with all them painters,' observed one child.

—

Just before Easter I was on playground duty and, knowing the mother of a nine-year-old girl was in hospital, I enquired how she was. 'She's fine,' she replied. 'She's coming home on Friday. She only went in for an Easter egg tummy.' (hysterectomy)

–

When I was teaching, six-year-old Alex was late for school one morning. I asked him why he was late. He replied, 'Mum's car broke down and she had to call the IRA to fix it.'

Questions and Answers

In 1984, when I was appointed general adviser for language development with Rotherham Local Education Authority, the first school on my list of visits was Broom Valley Infants. I was to examine and report on the teaching of reading.

There was a great feeling of anticipation that morning as I strolled up the drive of the infant school I had attended as a small child, in my dark inspectorial suit and black briefcase in hand. The school was no longer a vast and frightening place but just a small, square, featureless building, like so many post-war schools. I stood for a moment in the entrance hall staring down the corridor and thinking of my childhood, before informing the school secretary I had an appointment with the head-teacher. I took a deep breath. The smell of cabbage and floor polish had lingered – and so, I was soon to discover, had my teacher. Miss Greenhalgh was still there.

'I'm very pleased you have done so well, Gervase,' she told me. I ballooned with pride. 'Yes, you've done very well, very well indeed.' There was a short pause before Miss Greenhalgh added, 'Because you weren't on the top table, were you?'

She was right, I wasn't on the top table. But I did well in my examinations and went on to become an examiner myself. I was often amused by the unconscious humour of candidates. In response to one English Literature paper on the famous Shakespeare play, a candidate wrote: 'When Julius Caesar was on his way to the capital, he was set upon by a group of senators who were jealous of him and he was stabbed to death. His best friend was the last to stab the emperor and Caesar cried as he died: "Up yours, Brutus!".' One young hopeful, in response to a question about the character of Hamlet, wrote that 'he's a bit like the David Gower' and then wrote a masterful essay on the problems with the England cricket side.

chess

Epitaph

The school examiner, Mrs Best,
Who spent her life devising tests,
At last is sadly laid to rest,
And now in heaven *she's* assessed.

A question on a standardised reading test required children to place an appropriate word in the blank space: 'Pen is to ink as knife is to ...' One child wrote 'back'.

—

Question How would you make soft water hard?
Answer Freeze it.

—

Asked in a test what steroids were used for, one secondary-aged pupil wrote, 'They're the metal things which hold the stair carpet in place.'

—

Question Complete the following expression: 'Where there's a will ...'
Answer '... there's always a dead person.'

—

The numeracy test question in the national SAT tests asked the children to write answers in figures. Imagine my surprise when one of my pupils drew a string of matchstick men.

—

The SAT test paper in numeracy had a box, which said above: 'Show your working.'

One child had done an elaborate pencil sketch showing him busily working at his desk.

—

On a history test for children was the question : 'What do you know about Agricola?

One child answered, 'I know it is a fizzy drink for farmers.'

———

Answer on biology GCSE Paper: 'The appearance of the anus in evolution marked a massive breakthrough.'

———

On a Health and Safety Questionnaire:
Question 'What would you do if your little brother swallowed a key?'
Answer 'Get in through the window.'

———

The GCSE Chemistry paper asked: 'What advice would you give to someone handling dangerous chemicals?' The candidate's answer was nothing if succinct: 'Be careful.'

———

Question What is a myth?
Answer A female moth.

———

Question What proportion of the earth's surface is covered by sea?
Answer The blue bits.

———

Question What were the disadvantages of canal building?
Answer The bricks had to be built underwater.

———

The oil from the North Sea can also be used for frying chips.

———

During my lessons I get some of my work right and some of it wrong. Now I am getting most of my work right. Now my testes are much better.

———

'Can you name a bird with a long neck?' asked the teacher of her junior-aged class.

'Naomi Campbell,' came the prompt reply from the class wit.

———

Michelangelo spent most of his time on the ceiling.

———

Cleopatra's Needle was used to sew bodies into long white sheets and they became mummies.

———

I teach in a Yorkshire school and we were doing a project on the Tudors. I asked if anyone could recall the names of any of Henry VIII's wives.

'Well, there's Katherine of Harrogate and Ann of Leeds,' said one pupil.

———

Say briefly what you know about Lady Macbeth:

'She was a right old bitch.'

———

An inventive answer in an examination paper: 'When a bitch has puppies it's called alliteration.'

———

'What is the opposite of the word 'woe'?' asked the teacher

'Giddyup!' replied a pupil.

———

My young son, sitting the test to get into a prep school, was asked: 'What is the plural of deer?' He wrote 'darlings', His friend, asked to write the plural of 'spouse', wrote 'spice'. Both were successful, so I think the examiner recognised some imaginative potential.

—

'And with what do you connect Baden-Powell?' asked the teacher.

'A hyphen,' came the reply.

—

A simile is a colourful and interesting way of comparing things in poetry like 'she had a face like a sackful of dead ferrets.'

—

Eight-year-old: 'When the police catch a robber they put cuff links on him.'

—

A 'classic' is a really long and boring book that you have to read at school and sit an examination on.

—

Posthumous works of literature are those written after the author is dead.